TOOLS

Styrofoam Wreath

Wire Wreaths

Dry Oasis

Clippers

Wire Cutters

Hi/low melt glue gun

Glue Sticks

Design Knife

Straight Wires

Wrapping Wires

Scissors

Floral Tape

Greening Pins

Wired Picks

*I*t is impossible to imagine a world without flowers. We enjoy them in so many ways. They enliven and freshen a room, have a soothing effect on our senses, and their fragile forms inspire loving thoughts and tender feelings…a constant reminder of beauty and sweet pleasures. Dried floral arrangements are flowers that have faded into another form of usefulness.

When some flowers, grasses and leaves are dried they retain their perfume. Since the earliest of times petals and sweet scented rushes were strewn on floors, and filigree containers and cloth bags were filled with perfumed flora to sweeten drawers and cupboards. In the seventeenth century small packets of aromatic posies and scented dried leaves were carried to ward off the plague.

Interest in dried flora has fluctuated throughout the years, but since an extensive variety of dried flowers, grasses, leaves and the high/low melt glue gun have become available, imaginations have bloomed and enthusiasm has been kindled to revive the art of dried arrangements. This section of the book contains examples with instructions for making both traditional and non-traditional projects. If you can't find a plant you want, substitute with something similar in shape color and texture.

Materials

- *Ribbon*
- *Floral Wire*

BUTTON BOW

1 Cut a length of ribbon twice the streamer length (for one set of streamers).

FOR 6" STREAMERS CUT A 12" LENGTH OF RIBBON

2 Form a loop with the remaining ribbon and hold between thumb and index finger.

3 Continue forming loops in each direction.

THIS END BECOMES BUTTON LOOP

4 Before securing bow center with wire, add button loop to top by twisting the end of the tail on top of the bow (making sure the right side is out) over and under your thumb.

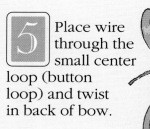

5 Place wire through the small center loop (button loop) and twist in back of bow.

6 Fan out the loops to make a full bow. To add the streamers, thread through loop and tie in back of bow. Repeat for as many streamers as desired.

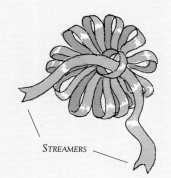

STREAMERS

LOOPY BOW

1 Make a loop leaving streamer the desired length.

STREAMER

2 Continue making loops keeping them uniform in size until bow is full and enough ribbon is left over to make remaining streamer.

3 Secure center of bow with wire and fan out.

Birds Nest Wreath

Materials

- *✿* 4" or 6" grapevine wreath
- *✿* 1 small mushroom bird
- *✿* Sphagnum moss
- *✿* Artemesia (natural)
- *✿* Broom bloom (burgundy)
- *✿* Larkspur (pink)
- *✿* Gyp (natural)
- *✿* 1/2 yard double-faced satin ribbon #1 1/2 pink

Instructions

1 Glue moss to the inside and front bottom section of the wreath.

2 Glue bird securely onto moss.

3 Glue small pieces of artemesia under and around the bird.

4 Glue small tips of broom bloom covering the area under the bird.

5 Break flowers from larkspur and glue as shown in photo..

6 Glue tips of gyp throughout the design to finish it.

7 Run the ribbon through the top of the wreath and tie a knot. Tie a bow after the knot and hang the wreath on a tree or pin it to the wall.

Decorated Hat

Materials

- *Straw hat*
- *3 yards french blue moire ribbon #9*
- *Spaghnum moss*
- *German statice (natural)*
- *Lavender flowers (natural)*
- *Globe amaranthus (pink)*
- *Larkspur (blue)*

Instructions

1 Leave a length of ribbon hanging from base of hat and glue it in place.

2 Loop the ribbon up off the hat an inch and glue it back down about 3 inches up the left side. Continue looping and gluing it all around the body of the hat every 3 inches. Finish by crossing the ribbon over the first glued down area allowing the end to form a second tail off the rim of the hat.

3 Glue moss over the glued spots on the ribbon.

4 Break off pieces of statice and glue them facing in all directions on the mossy areas.

5 Glue lavender flowers lightly on the mossy areas and heavily where the ribbon crosses over at the tail.

6 Glue 3 or 4 globe amaranthus to each area using a few extra at the ribbon tails.

7 Glue larkspur flowers to different areas filling in any blank spaces.

Bird's Branch

Materials

- 2 small or 1 large lichen covered oak branch (manzanita, birch or curly willow can be substituted)
- Sphaghnum moss
- 2 medium size mushroom birds
- 1 small birds nest
- Brisa (natural)
- Mint flowers (pink)
- Larkspur (blue)

Instructions

1 Break the branches or arrange them so that one end has the stems cut off evenly and the other end branches out in several directions. Rubber band the blunt ends together about 2 to 3 inches up the stem.

2 Tuck some moss into the rubber band and glue moss around it. Glue several patches of moss on the rest of the stems.

3 Glue birds nest with bird near base of stems and another bird further up the stems.

4 Glue pieces of brisa under the nest, the second bird and all over the mossy areas.

5 Break the flowers from the mint stem, and glue them on the mossy areas using the larger flowers towards the base and a few smaller ones further up the branches.

6 Fill in the design with flowers from the larkspur stem.

Materials

- 2 yards dark green paper ribbon
- Celosia (burgundy)
- Roses (fire and ice)
- Latifolia (natural)
- Sch (natural)
- Larkspur (dark blue)

Instructions

1 Unfold paper ribbon until flat.

2 Fold ribbon in half and tie a bow in the center of the yardage. Cross tails over each other to form one solid tail. Secure tail at bottom by gluing together about 3" from bottom.

3 Glue moss lightly down center of tail to cross-over.

4 Break celosia into small pieces and glue onto moss every inch or two.

5 Glue on the rose heads spreading them out evenly.

6 Glue on tips of latifolia covering the moss heavily.

7 Glue tips of sch facing upwards and downwards along length of tail.

8 Fill in all the empty spaces with small florets of larkspur.

VICTORIAN WREATH

Materials

- ✽ *12" styrofoam wreath form*
- ✽ *Spaghnum moss and greening pins*
- ✽ *Wild gyp (natural)*
- ✽ *Broom bloom (navy)*
- ✽ *Tree fern (green)*
- ✽ *Floral buttons (warm blue)*
- ✽ *Sch (natural)*
- ✽ *Dried roses (pink)*
- ✽ *Celosia (burgundy)*

Instructions

1 Cover all sides of wreath, except back, with moss. Secure moss with greening pins every 2" or so.

2 Break off pieces of gyp and push directly into the wreath. Begin on the lower outside and filling in the full circle. Then work your way to the inside. Place each branch of gyp very close to the last one forming almost a solid mass of gyp over the entire wreath.

3 Break broom bloom into small pieces and push into wreath in clusters. Alternate back and forth around wreath forming an evenly distributed pattern.

4 Add clumps of tree fern following the same method. For the fern, some gluing may be required to secure it.

5 Insert 3 or 4 button stems at a time alternating back and forth. Fill in empty spaces in gyp.

6 Glue in sch 1 or 2 at a time using same method.

7 Add roses around center of wreath one at a time.

8 Break celosia into small clumps and glue into gyp all around wreath.

9 Glue in blooms of globe amaranthus all around wreath until you reach desired fullness.

CHERUB WITH BOUQUET

Materials

- Terra-cotta cherub (medium size sitting with arms crossed over lap)
- Mini rose buds (mauve)
- Plumosa (green)
- Latifolia (natural)

Instructions

Head Wreath

1 Remove roses from stem. Place a small dot of glue on one side of rose and set on outside perimeter of the cherubs head. Continue gluing each rose bud the same way placing end to end around the outside of the head forming a wreath shape as you go.

Arm Bouquet

1 Glue plumosa into arms forming the shape of the bouquet. The greens should poke out under the left arm and cross over the lap coming up and over the right arm.

2 Glue in tips of latifolia following the shape of the greens.

3 Finish by gluing in rose buds throughout the greens and filler.

Decorated Basket Handle

Materials

✿ *Medium size basket with a handle*

✿ *2 yards dark green french wired ribbon #9*

✿ *6 dried roses (white)*

✿ *Larkspur (pink)*

Instructions

1 Glue end of ribbon to inside rim of basket handle.

2 Wrap ribbon loosely around handle. Cut at rim of other side and glue to inside of handle.

3 Cut remaining yardage of ribbon in half and tie a bow around the base of each handle facing outward.

4 Glue 3 roses to each side placing 1 rose above the bow and 2 roses below the bow.

5 Accent roses with small larkspur flowers using 3 or 4 blooms on each side.

NATURE'S BOUNTY BASKET

Materials

- Low flat basket
- 1/2 brick dry oasis
- Spaghnum moss and greening pins
- Larkspur (blue)
- Brisa media (natural)
- Mint flowers (natural)
- Peonies (natural)
- Papaver (natural) 'poppy pods'
- Liatrus (natural)
- Globe amaranthus (pink)
- Sage (natural)
- Marjoram (natural)
- Roses (fire and ice)
- Australian daisies (natural)

Instructions

1 Cut brick of oasis length wise down center. Glue to bottom of basket and cover with moss, securing moss with greening pins every 2" or so.

2 Arrange 2 or 3 pieces of larkspur in your hand, staggering the heights. Cut stems even at the bottom and push into oasis towards the back left corner of basket. Repeat 4 or 5 times until a clump is formed.

3 Add stems of brisa, using the same method, next to larkspur in center back area of basket. Overlap with larkspur only slightly.

4 Add full stems of mint filling in back right area of basket. Place the mint a little higher than the brisa, almost as tall as the larkspur. Add a very small clump of mint to the far left of the basket next to the larkspur.

5 Place each peony stem in one at a time. Start with the tallest bloom half way up the larkspur clump, then stagger down to 2 or 3 inches above the rim of the basket. Glue the extra peony leaves around the base of each peony stem as they would grow naturally.

6 Place each liatrus stem in the same way beginning next to the peonies with the tallest stem towards the top of the brisa.

7 Add the pods next using the same method. Beginning height should be between the peonies and larkspur heights. Place them in front of the mint. Also place 4 to 6 pods in far left front corner in front of larkspur.

8 Put in whole stems of amaranthus next to pods in front of mint. Begin lower than the pods and fill in the remaining end of the basket..

9 Finish that side of basket by adding clumps of sage in front and among the amaranthus down to the very rim of the basket

10 Next to the sage, finish the area in front of the poppies and liatrus by using short pieces of larkspur. Place the top pieces upward and the lower pieces outward down to the rim of the basket.

11 Finish area in-between and under peonies with marjoram. Some gluing may be needed.

12 Place roses next to peonies under larkspur and mint. Stagger the heights down to the rim of the basket.

13 Finish far left side with Australian daisies. Stagger heights from just under mint through roses and down to the rim of the basket.

Small Accent Wreath

Materials

- 6" Grapevine wreath
- Spaghnum moss (optional)
- Plumosa fern (green)
- Rose heads (pink)
- Mint (natural)
- Floral buttons (warm blue)
- Larkspur (white)
- Statice sinuata (purple)
- Latifolia (natural)

Instructions

1 Glue moss all over front of wreath.

2 Glue fern tips every inch or so.

3 Glue on rose heads (cluster if preferred).

4 Break mint flowers apart and glue evenly around wreath.

5 Glue buttons alternating side to side.

6 Break flowers from stem of larkspur and glue in place.

7 Add small pieces of statice filling in blank areas..

8 Fill in remaining blank areas with tips of latifolia.

POTTED WHEAT BUNDLE

Materials

- Tarwe (natural)
- 1/4 brick dry oasis
- 5" terra-cotta pot
- Sphagnum moss
- 1 yard navy blue french wired ribbon #5
- Celosia (burgundy)

Instructions

1 Cut edges off dry oasis to round off the square.

2 Push oasis into pot and cut off top of oasis so that it is flush with the top of the pot.

3 Cover the oasis with moss, leaving the center open.

4 Arrange wheat bundle in your hand so that all hulls are at the same height.

5 Cut the wheat stems off evenly at the bottom to the desired height. Hold the bottoms of the stems together and firmly push the entire bundle into the oasis.

6 Cover any oasis still showing with more moss.

7 About half way from the top and bottom, tie the stems together firmly with the ribbon, knotting the ribbon first and then tying a simple bow.

8 Glue a few small pieces of celosia above and below the bow and around the base of the wheat bunch.

NOTE: Arrangement can be used as is or placed in decorative container as shown in photo.

Wall Swag

Materials

- ❧ Styrofoam wreath or block
- ❧ Sphagnum moss and greening pins
- ❧ Larkspur (pink)
- ❧ Sprengerii fern (green)
- ❧ 3 yards mauve wired moire ribbon #9
- ❧ Peonies (natural)
- ❧ Lavender flowers (natural)
- ❧ Celosia (burgundy)
- ❧ Broom Bloom (Burgundy)

Instructions

1 Cut styrofoam into a 6" x 3" piece.

2 Cover all sides except back with moss securing with greening pins every 2" or so.

3 Insert larkspur into foam. Start with the longest pieces on the outside at the maximum desired length. Add more pieces coming in shorter and shorter to center. Leave the exact center empty, but larkspur should be fanning out in either direction from the empty center.

4 Add sprengerii, starting just inside the longest pieces of larkspur and working towards the center.

5 Stretch length of ribbon across center of swag with each end 3 to 4 inches inside of longest pieces of larkspur. Secure in the middle with a greening pin.

6 Make a 4 loop bow with remaining ribbon and secure with wire. Push wire down through center of ribbon length and foam.

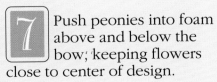

7 Push peonies into foam above and below the bow, keeping flowers close to center of design.

8 Glue peony leaves around flowers following same outward design.

9 Glue stems of lavender in clumps of 3-5 blooms with the longest stems towards the outside and shorter and tighter stems towards the center.

10 Break celosia into small pieces and glue evenly throughout swag.

11 Glue in small tips of broom bloom evenly throughout swag filling in any blank spaces.

Dried Fruit Basket

Materials

- *Flat basket without a handle*
- *1/4 brick dry oasis*
- *Sphagnum moss and greening pins*
- *5 grapefruit slices*
- *4 red pomegranates*
- *7 orange slices*
- *8 apple slices*
- *Silk berry clusters*

Instructions

1 Secure oasis to basket in back left corner.

2 Cover oasis with moss, securing with greening pins.

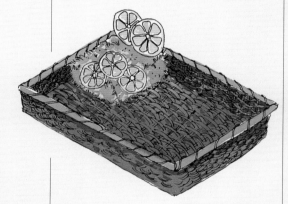

3 Glue in slices of grapefruit, two standing and three laying on their sides. Secure each slice with a greening pin.

4 Glue the bottoms of each pomegranate and place around grapefruit slices.

5 Glue oranges away from grapefruit filling in the space on the oasis..

6 Glue in apple slices between citrus alternating colors and textures. Some should be upright and some can be on their sides.

7 Finish by adding the silk berry clusters around fruit and cascading onto rim of basket.

Victorian Tussy Mussy

Materials

- Lace bridal bouquet backing
- Bloom broom (navy)
- Roses (pink)
- Floral buttons (burgundy)
- Mint flowers (pink)
- Globe amaranthus (pink)

Instructions

1 Create a dome of bloom broom above the lace and flush with the lace. Begin by passing full stems through the center hole of the lace and gluing smaller pieces onto the sides and filling in the blank spaces. Leave the stems long so they create the balance of stems for the bouquet.

2 Using the same method add the roses. If necessary, glue the roses in the side areas and glue the stems to the bottom of the bouquet.

3 Place 2 rose leaves around each rose bloom.

4 Glue in each button spreading them evenly throughout the bouquet.

5 Break apart mint flowers and glue in each blossom following the same method.

6 Glue in globe amaranthus the same until you reach desired fullness.

7 Finish by tying a length of ribbon around the stems just below the lace doily and letting the bow tails hang down longer than the stems.

Materials

- *Sprengerii fern (green)*
- *Larkspur (pink)*
- *Broom bloom (burgundy)*
- *2 yards mauve wired moire ribbon #9*

Instructions

1 Lay out 3 pieces of fern with the center piece being the longest.

2 Lay out 3 pieces broom bloom over the fern but back 3-4 inches with the center piece being the longest.

3 Lay out 3 pieces of larkspur over the broom bloom but back another 3 inches again, with the center piece being the longest.

4 Following the same procedure, add another layer of fern.

5 Add only 1 piece of broom bloom over the fern.

6 Add another 3-4 pieces of larkspur. Continue adding layers staggering the length shorter and shorter until you have reached the ends of the first stems added.

7 Rubber band the stems together leaving 2-3 inches exposed at the top.

8 Tie the ribbon over the rubber band and knot it tight. Tie a simple bow and hang the bouquet on the wall with the bow on the top.

Decorated Basket

Materials

- *Basket with or without handle*
- *Spaghnum moss*
- *German statice (natural)*
- *Floral buttons (burgundy)*
- *Globe amaranthus (pink)*
- *Larkspur (pink)*
- *Broom bloom (blue)*
- *Statice sinuata (purple)*

Instructions

1 Glue moss down covering the rim of the basket.

2 Glue tips of German statice to moss facing all the tips in the same direction.

3 Glue buttons to moss every inch or so along rim of the basket.

4 Glue heads of amaranthus to moss spreading out evenly.

5 Break flowers from stem of larkspur and glue onto moss all around basket.

6 Break small clusters of tips from the broom bloom and glue onto moss covering empty spaces.

7 Fill in remaining empty spaces with small blooms of sinuata statice.

8 Fill the rim of the basket to the desired fullness and feel free to add any other flowers, pods or 'scraps' you choose.

Basket of Herbs

Materials

- Vine 'birds nest' basket
- 1/8 brick dry oasis
- Spaghnum moss and greening pins
- Artemesia (natural)
- Sage (natural)
- Marjoram (natural)
- Lavender (natural)
- Mint flowers (natural)
- Globe amaranthus (pink)
- Australian daisy (natural)

Instructions

1 Glue oasis to bottom of basket.

2 Cover oasis on all sides with moss securing with greening pins every 2" or so.

3 Arrange 3-4 stems of artemesia in your hand staggering the heights. Cut the bottoms off evenly and push into oasis towards far left side of basket. Use these tall herbs to set the perimeter of the design. Place another clump at the other end of the basket, low and facing outward. Place several more clumps throughout the basket moving out in all directions.

4 Add in the marjoram in the same type clumps, spread evenly, around the basket and creating the outer line of the arrangement.

5 Follow the same method adding in the sage.

6 Add the lavender to the arrangement using the same method. Be sure as you go to keep filling in the empty spaces and staying within the outer line of the arrangement.

7 Add the stems of mint one at a time spreading hem evenly through the basket and again filling in the empty spaces.

8 To add the globe amaranthus and the Australian daisies, you will need to use some hot glue. Break the stems to the desired length and place a dab of glue on the bottom of the stem. Push the stem into the area you want and hold for a minute. The last stems of flowers should fill in the arrangement and some can be layered on top of other flowers or greens.

Growing Your Own

Growing your own flowers gives you the added enjoyment of appreciating them while they are fresh as well as dried. You don't need a large area to grow enough plants for several large arrangements. Plan your garden so you can enjoy it year round by planting evergreens, deciduous plants, annuals and perennials. A variety of colors, shapes and textures will provide material for interesting projects without leaving the garden barren when you cut for drying. Plant rows of flowers in your vegetable garden. Herbs are easy to grow and delicately scent a room when used in a wreath or arrangement.

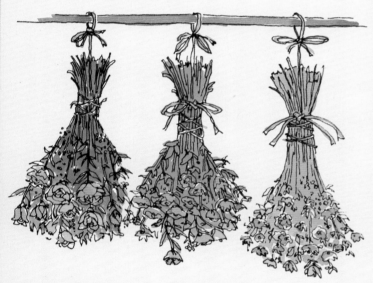

Harvesting

Success depends not only upon extracting all the moisture from the plant material but also on picking the plants at the right time. Cut flowers when the heads feel firm and before they come into full bloom. Enjoy cut roses as they open, and when they reach a full stage remove them from the water and hang them upside down to dry. Line flowers like delphinium, larkspur, foxgloves, lupins etc., should be gathered when the lower buds are flowering, but the top ones have not yet bloomed. Choose perfect plants. Avoid cutting before the morning dew has dried off, after rainfall and before the mid-day sun has begun to wilt them. Gather more than you need to allow

for breakage. Stalks should be cut at an angle with sharp clippers or scissors.

Air Drying

This is the simplest and most commonly used method for a wide variety of flowers, herbs, gourds, grasses, leafy branches, seedheads and cereals. Most flowers can be tied in small bunches with raffia or string and hung upside down. Stagger the heads so as not to crowd and to help prevent rot. Bunches should contain one type of flower. Hang in a warm, dry place away from direct sunlight in a spare room, attic, cellar, garage, shed...any dry area with circulating air. You can use wall hooks poles or wires placed at least 6" from the ceiling.

Sturdy flowers like bells of Ireland, roses, statice, gypsophylia, yarrow and larkspur dry particularly well using the air-dry method. Strip off all the leaves and thorns first, because they retain moisture and will slow down the drying process. The faster flowers dry the more color they retain. Also, when they dry quickly they aren't as fragile. Dry large flowers individually.

The flower heads of many of the straw flowers are too heavy for the dried stems to support. Cut off the stems and wire them before hanging up to dry.

CREATE A WIRE STEM AND WRAP WITH FLORIST TAPE

Grasses, moss, lichen, bamboo, fungi and leafy branches dry well when laid flat on an absorbent surface such as cardboard, newspaper or even wooden floorboards. Whole branches, ferns, bracken and spiky leaves can be dried this way. Arrange material in a single layer on several pieces of newspaper without overlapping. The leaves will shrivel a little but retain their color and natural shape on the stalk, which they don't do if they are hung upside down or dried upright.

Many tall grasses dry well standing up in a dry vase. Be sure to seal pampas grass, bulrushes and other seed heads by spraying them with hair spray or a similar fixative before drying, so they don't fall apart.

Make a simple shelf of coarse gauge chicken wire for air drying heavy headed plant material such as globe artichokes, large onion seedheads, protea, and large thistles. Each plant has a home in a hole. Make enough room beneath to allow the stalk to hang freely.

Water Drying

Flowers such as proteas, heathers, yarrow, hybrid delphiniums, acacia, hydrangeas, gypsophila and mimosa dry well when left standing in a vase with 2" of water and left until the water disappears and the plants are dry.

Preserving

Miniature oak, maple and magnolia leaves, eucalyptus, copper beech, pin oak, laurel, ferns and ivy can be dried successfully by leaving them stand in a solution of glycerine and water. The color of the leaves usually changes from green to a beautiful, rich shade of greenish brown. Gather the foliage in the summer while the sap is still rising.

Cut the base of each stalk at a sharp angle so the plant will take up the mixture quickly. Remove leaves from the bottom so that only the stem rests in the solution. Hardwood stems should be hammered and split.

Stand the plants in water for a couple of hours so they are refreshed. Then make the glycerine solution using 40% glycerine and 60% very hot water. Stand the plants in a container with 3-4" of the mixture in the bottom. Leave in a cool, dark place for about 10 days.

As the glycerine is absorbed through the plant, it becomes embalmed so that it is dried yet still supple. Material treated with glycerine lasts indefinitely and can be dusted or wiped with a damp cloth without risk.

Oven Drying

Compact flowers such as marigold, chrysanthemums, cornflowers and zinnias dry well in a ventilated oven. They retain their color and shape. The material must be dried at a very low temperature (150 degrees) over many hours. Flowers are slotted through holes in a wire mesh rack with room for the stalks to hang freely. The time required depends on how dense or porous the flowers are. Check often to make sure the oven doesn't get too hot. Fan assisted ovens are most suitable for this method because other types generate too much moisture.

Microwave Drying

Sunflowers, chrysanthemums, roses, asters, zinnias...any compact flower dries well and retains its color and shape when dried in the microwave. Individual leaves, leaf sprays and pine cones also dry well with this method. Fresh, perfect, half open flowers are best.

Place a layer of silica gel crystals in a large cup and stand the flower upright in the crystals. Gently cover the flower completely. Place the cup in a microwave on High for 1 minute 20 seconds. Remove a few crystals to check if the petals are still soft. If they are, re-cover the flower and microwave in 15 second timings until the flower is dry. Pour the silica gel out into a bowl and stand the flower with its base in the hot crystals for a few minutes. Brush off the crystals with an artists brush and the flower is ready for wiring.

Dessicants

Though drying with dessicants, such as silica gel or a mixture of borax and cornmeal, can be the least predictable way to preserve flowers and foliage the results can be dazzling and life-like. The dessicant must be completely dry before you begin. Warm it in the oven for a half hour, then place a layer in the bottom of a plastic storage box.

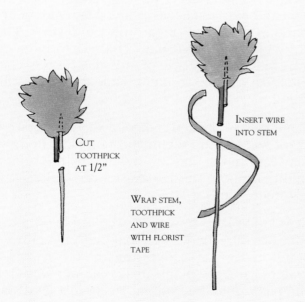

CUT TOOTHPICK AT 1/2"

INSERT WIRE INTO STEM

WRAP STEM, TOOTHPICK AND WIRE WITH FLORIST TAPE

Cut the stem of a flower 1" from the base of the head, insert a wooden toothpick into the base and trim the toothpick to 1/2". After the flower is dried a wire can be inserted into the stem and taped with floral tape to form a flexible stem.

Cut off the flower heads leaving a 1" stem (for future wiring). Pour a blanket of silica gel or an equal mixture of borax and cornmeal over each flower separating the petals carefully with a toothpick as you pour. When each flower is completely covered, put a tight fitting lid on the container and store in a dry place. Check in 4-5 days to see if the flowers are papery. If not, cover and check again in a couple of days. If they are left too long in silica gel they become brittle and dark, so check frequently. When dry brush off desiccant with a soft artist brush and wire the stem.

To restore silica gel for re-use, preheat oven to 300 degrees. Sift through to remove as much left-over plant material as possible and spread a single layer of it on the bottom of a shallow pan. Stir every so-often until it regains its original blue color. Store after cooling in an air-tight container.

Pressing

Delicate flowers like pansies, lace-cap hydrangeas, lilies, freesia, anemones, hellebore, marguerites, primroses, snowdrops, clematis, ferns and tree leaves or sprays are perfect for pressing between the pages of an out-dated phone book.

Flowers can also be dried between sheets of absorbent paper and placed under a couple of heavy books. Larger pieces of foliage can be pressed between sheets of newspaper and placed under a little used area of carpet. The length of time material takes to dry depends on how porous or dense it is, check after 10 days.

Pressed flowers retain their color and shape and are perfect for personalized greeting cards, stationery, pictures and for decorating lampshades.

PREPARING BOWLS, SAUCERS AND VASES

Bowls

Shape some foam to fit the bowl. Using waterproof clay, secure a plastic frog on the bottom of the bowl. Impale the foam on the frog.

Dishes

Mound the top of the foam using extra pieces taped together if necessary. Using a strong glue, adhere the foam to the dish.

Tall Vases

Using oasis foam, stuff entire vase with pieces of foam that extend about an inch above the top of the vase.

Spherical Vases

Insert a loose ball of chicken wire inside, and stretch it until it pushes against the interior surfaces.

Glass containers

Adhere plastic frogs to the bottom of the glass container with adhesive clay. Cut the foam about 3/4" from all four sides of the vase. Secure the foam on the frogs and fill the edges of the vase with potpourri using wire or sticks to ease the petals into the space. You can also use lichen and moss to cover the foam.

Pebbles and stones can be used to camouflage stems in glass containers or to add weight so the vase won't topple over.

Preparing a Basket

If you choose to paint your basket, spray paints are fast and easy, but poster paints and water based colors produce a subtler effect. A final coat of clear polyurethane varnish will enrich the natural colors and add gloss.

Securing the Foam

If the arrangement is small and balanced the foam will usually stay in place with a glob of hot glue, or you can impale it on a plastic frog that has been adhered to the bottom of the basket with adhesive clay. For larger arrangements wire and adhesive tape work well.

You will need enough dry foam to mound over the top of the basket, a sharp knife, sphagnum moss, narrow florist adhesive tape and medium gauge wire.

1. Using the base of the basket, imprint a block of foam.

2. Using the impression from the basket as a pattern, cut the foam to fit inside the basket snugly.

3. If you need more foam for height, round the top of another piece and place it on top of the first foam. Then, form a small loop at the end of a piece of wire, thread some florist tape through it and poke the wire through the basket on the inside of the rim (like a needle threader).

4. Pull enough tape through to reach the other side and unthread the "needle". Leaving about 1 1/2" on each side of the tape to stick back on itself. Trim. You may need additional strips of tape over the top of the foam to hold it firmly if the basket is large.

5. Cover the foam with a thin layer of moss.

Making Your Own Style Container or Baskets

If you have access to some fresh hay you can easily make a charming container for a dried floral arrangement. You won't find hay in a craft store, but depending on where you live and what time of year you are looking for it, hay shouldn't be too difficult to locate.

Gather a basket, vase, or can, some long strips of raffia and enough hay to give the container a thick covering.

Place hay on top of two long strips of raffia, and roll the basket using the raffia to hold the hay in place.

Tie the raffia tightly adding additional strips if needed and trim the top.

Anchor foam inside by adhering a plastic frog to the bottom of the basket with adhesive clay and inserting the foam into the frog. Hide the mechanics with moss.

Florists and craft stores sell styrofoam bases which you can cover with a thick coating of moss held in place with 'u' shaped pins; vine wreaths you can glue things onto or stick things through and wire frames you can cover in the following way.

Preparing a Standard Wire Frame

1. Spray some mossy plant material with water. Using a commercial wire frame, attach the end of a ball of twine to the inner wire ring. Place a clump of moss on top of the frame and wind the ball of twine around it in several places.

2. Overlap clumps of moss binding as you go. Maintain an even thickness.

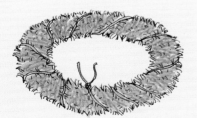

3. When you have come full circle, find the original knot end, cut the twine and tie the ends together. Allow wreath to dry thoroughly (up to a week) before gluing on the dried flowers.

Making Your Own Chicken Wire and Moss Wreath Base

When you know how to make your own wreath base you aren't limited to the sizes available in the stores.

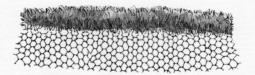

1. Cut a piece of chicken wire 1' wide and however long you need to make the size wreath you want. Lay it flat and arrange damp moss along one edge.

2. Roll the wire tightly to form a solid tube about 1 1/2" thick. Tuck in moss and wires as you go.

3. Gradually ease it into a circle. Don't overlap the ends. They are sewn together by attaching reel wire to one end and "sewing" the two ends of the tube together. Tie and conceal the ends of the wire.

Hanging Loop

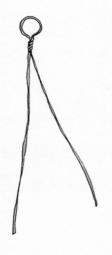

1. Cover a piece of medium gauge wire with floral tape and twist a circle in the middle.

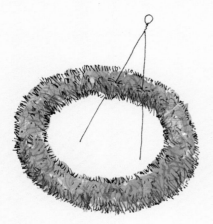

2. Push the end of the wire into the back of the covered wreath base.

3. Secure the ends by pushing them into the moss on each side of the back of the wreath.

Dried Floral Trees

Small trees made with real branches and tree shaped dry foam are very easy to construct and make beautiful, bonsai-like arrangements.

You will need a sturdy base to support your tree. Plaster of Paris dries quickly and provides the weight you need to keep your tree stable.

1. First line a small pot with slivers of dry foam. Plaster of Paris expands as it sets. The foam acts a cushion and keeps the pot from cracking.

2. Mix enough plaster of Paris and water to fill the pot 2/3 full. Make sure the slivers of foam stay in place as you spoon the mixture into the pot.

3. Insert a branch for a trunk making sure it rests on the bottom of the pot. Turn the pot to make sure the trunk looks good from all angles. When you are happy with it add some more plaster to within a 1/2 inch of the rim.

4. When the plaster is dry impale a foam cone on the trunk, and cover it with moss using 'u' pins or pieces of wire shaped into 'u's to hold the moss in place.

5. Decorate by pushing whatever flora you like into the foam. You can wedge the small pot into a more decorative container if you like. Cover the mechanics with moss.

Creating a long graceful swag to adorn a banister, doorway, shelves, fireplace, wall or table is an investment in time but a constant reminder of special events. A wire based swag is flexible, strong and easy to make.

1. Unroll enough reel wire for the length of the swag you want to make. Don't cut the wire. Make a loop at the end (to be used for hanging). Wire a small bouquet and trim the ends so they are even.

2. Place the bouquet on top of the wire covering the loop and bind it in place with the attached reel of wire. Pass the reel under the last loop of binding and pull tight.

3. Make a second bunch of flowers the same size as the first, and place it on the wire with the tips covering the binding of the first bouquet. Bind the second bouquet in place as you did the first one. Repeat until the swag is completed

Wheat

Floral Buttons

Air dry rose

Broom Bloom

Broom Bloom

Larkspur

Floral Buttons

Marjoram

Sage

Liatrus

Gypsophelia

Latifolia

THE BEST
DRIED FLOWER BOOK

THE BEST DRIED FLOWER BOOK
ISBN 1-56824-050-3

9 781568 240503

01295

■ MARK
PUBLISHING

5400 SCOTTS VALLEY DR.
SCOTTS VALLEY, CA 95066
ISBN 1-56824-050-3